Welcome to a gallery of creative G letters. These black and white Gs are just waiting for you to color.

Whether you use markers, pencils or another medium use an extra paper backing your work in case color bleeds through. The colorized Gallery gives some examples of how you can color them. Feel free to make your own color choices if you wish.

All these G letters were hand designed by artist Peggy Louise Parrish. If you want to make a few "in house" copies for yourself to try different colors you have her permission. Maybe you will have new ideas for letter G from this book adventure.

Enjoy!

Welcome to the Gorgeous Letter G

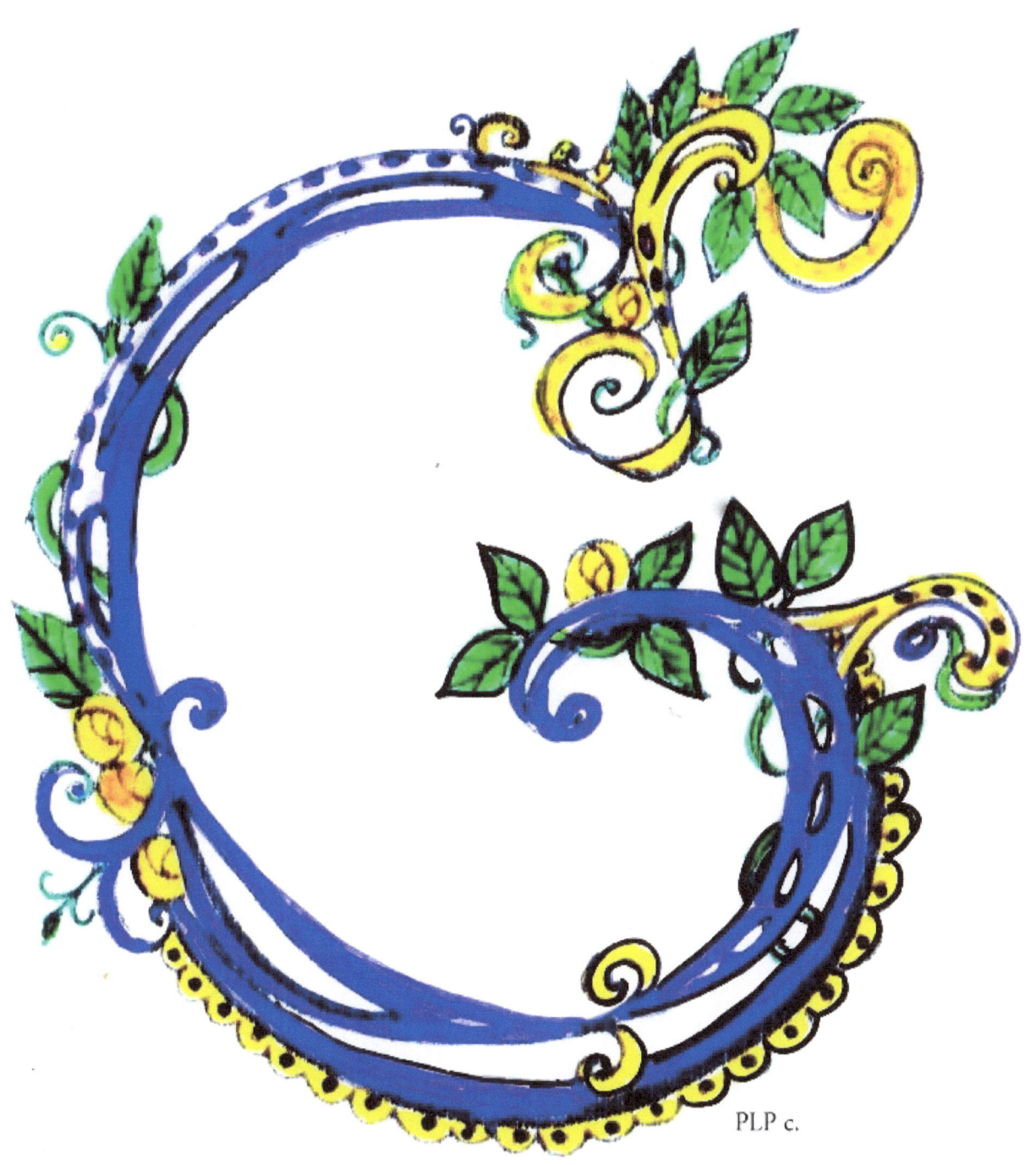

PLP c.

The Gorgeous Letter G Coloring Book

By Peggy Louise Parrish

C. 2017

Gorgeous Letter G

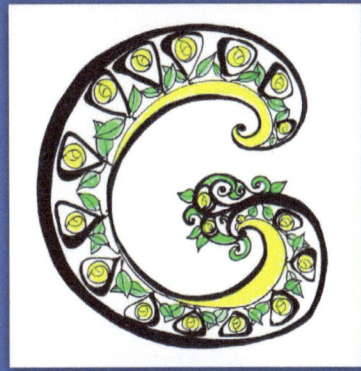
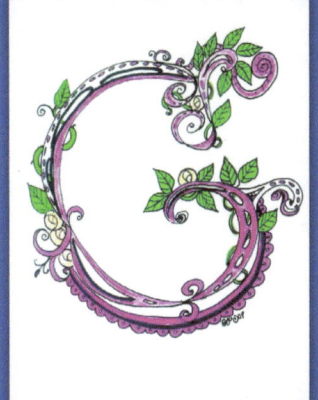
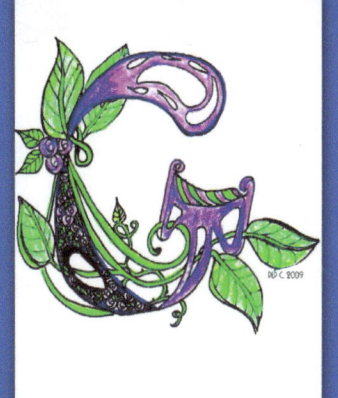

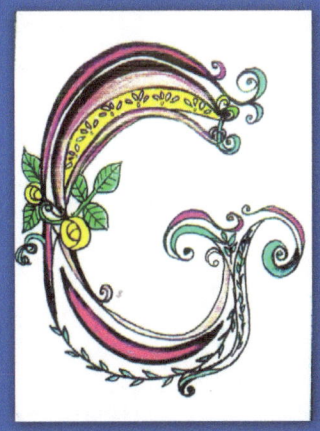
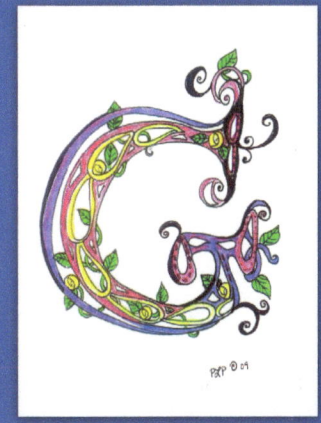
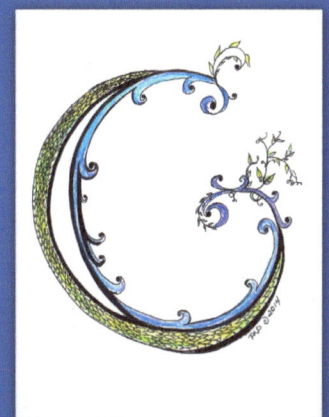

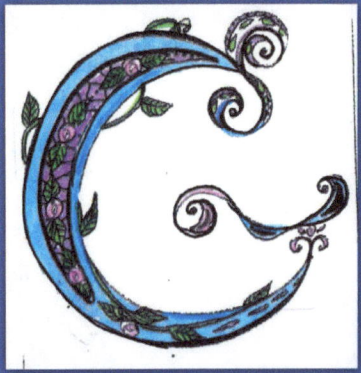
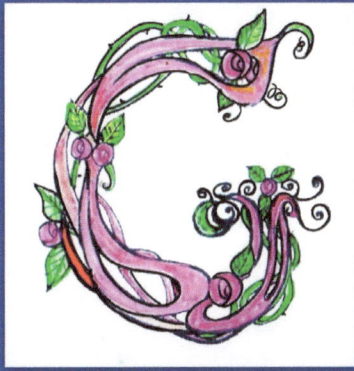
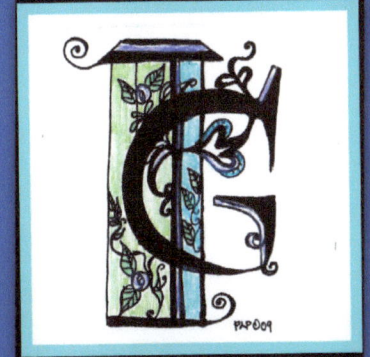

By Artist Peggy Louise Parrish

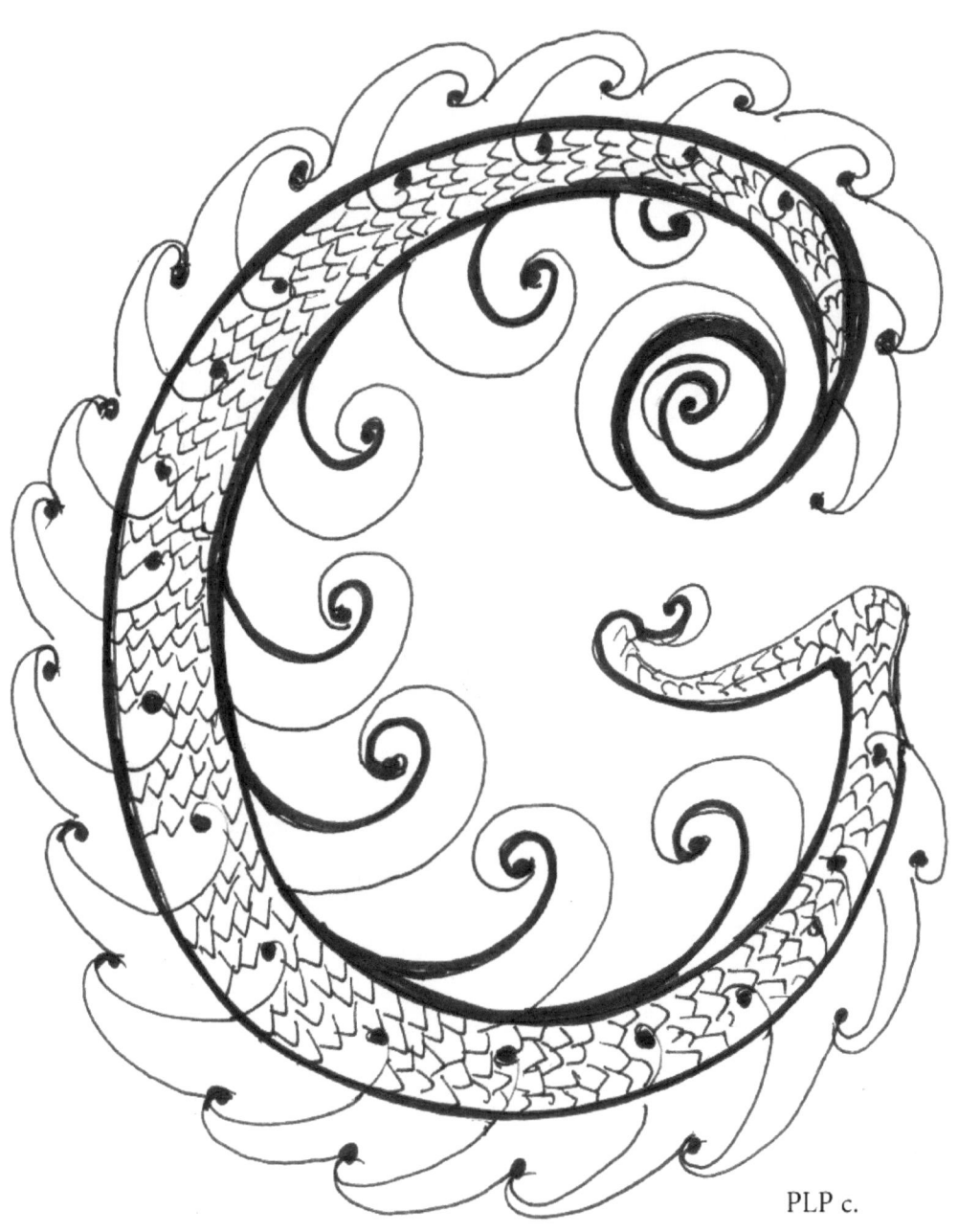

PLP c.

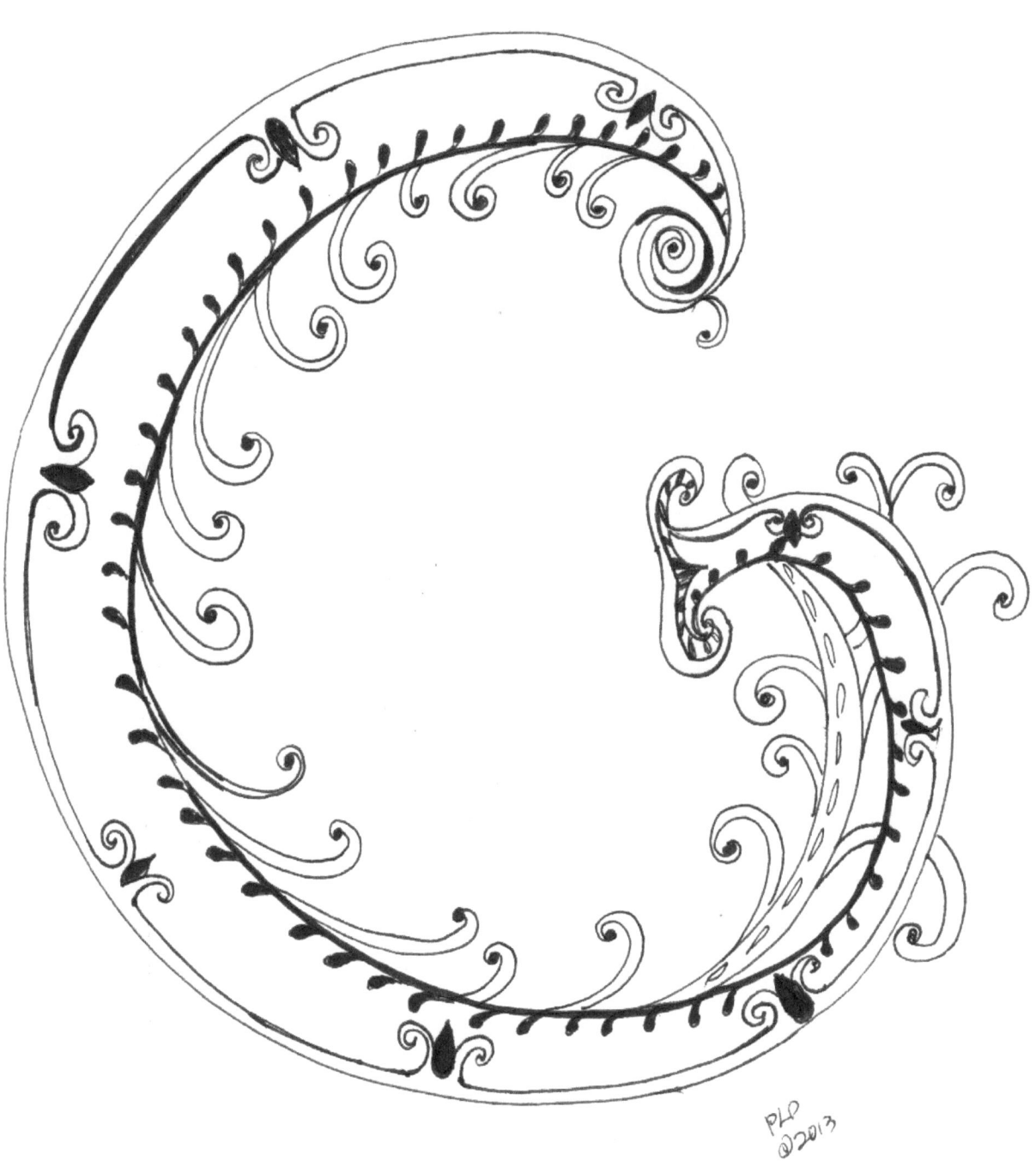

PLP
@2013

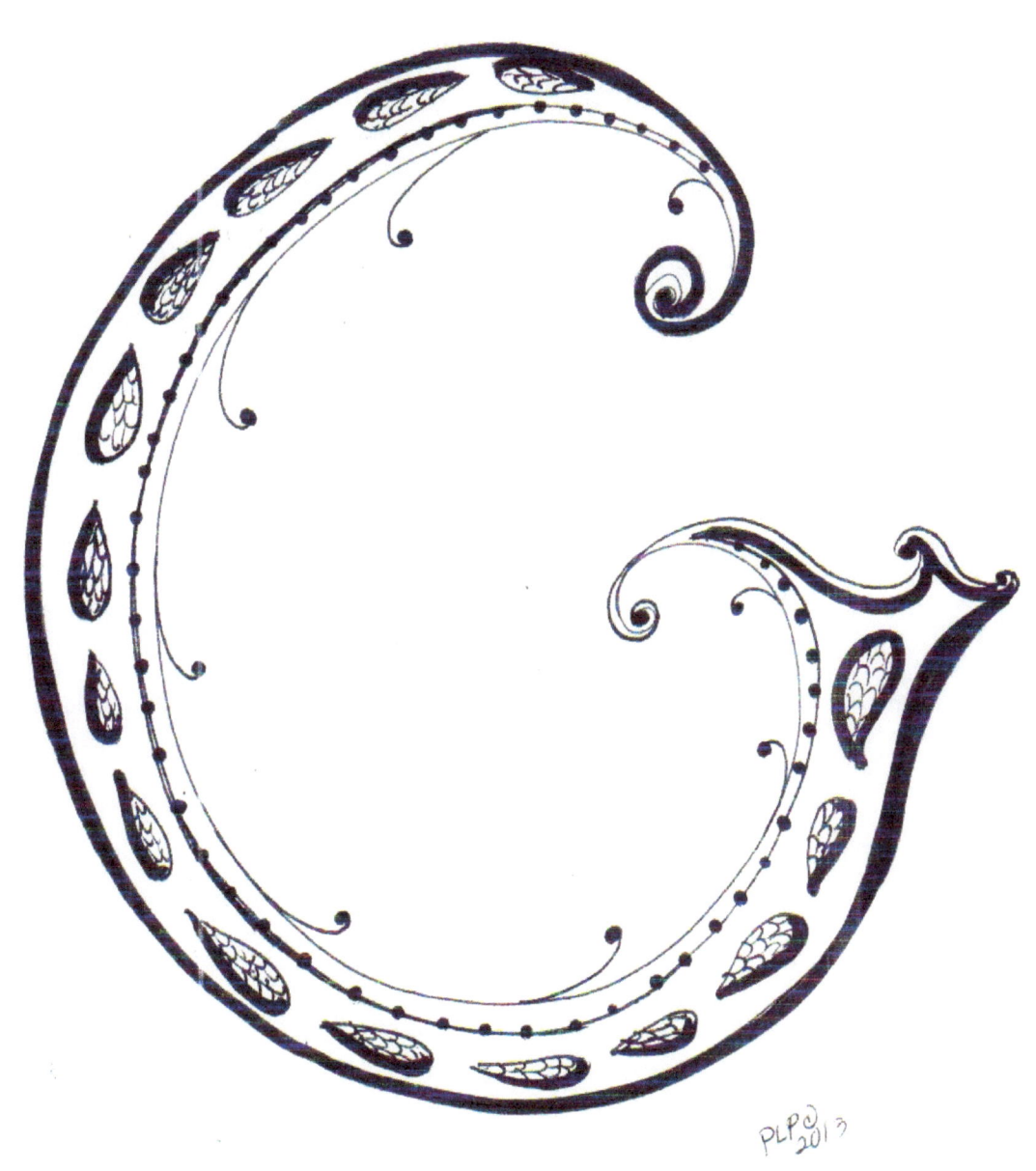

PLP©
2013

PLP cl

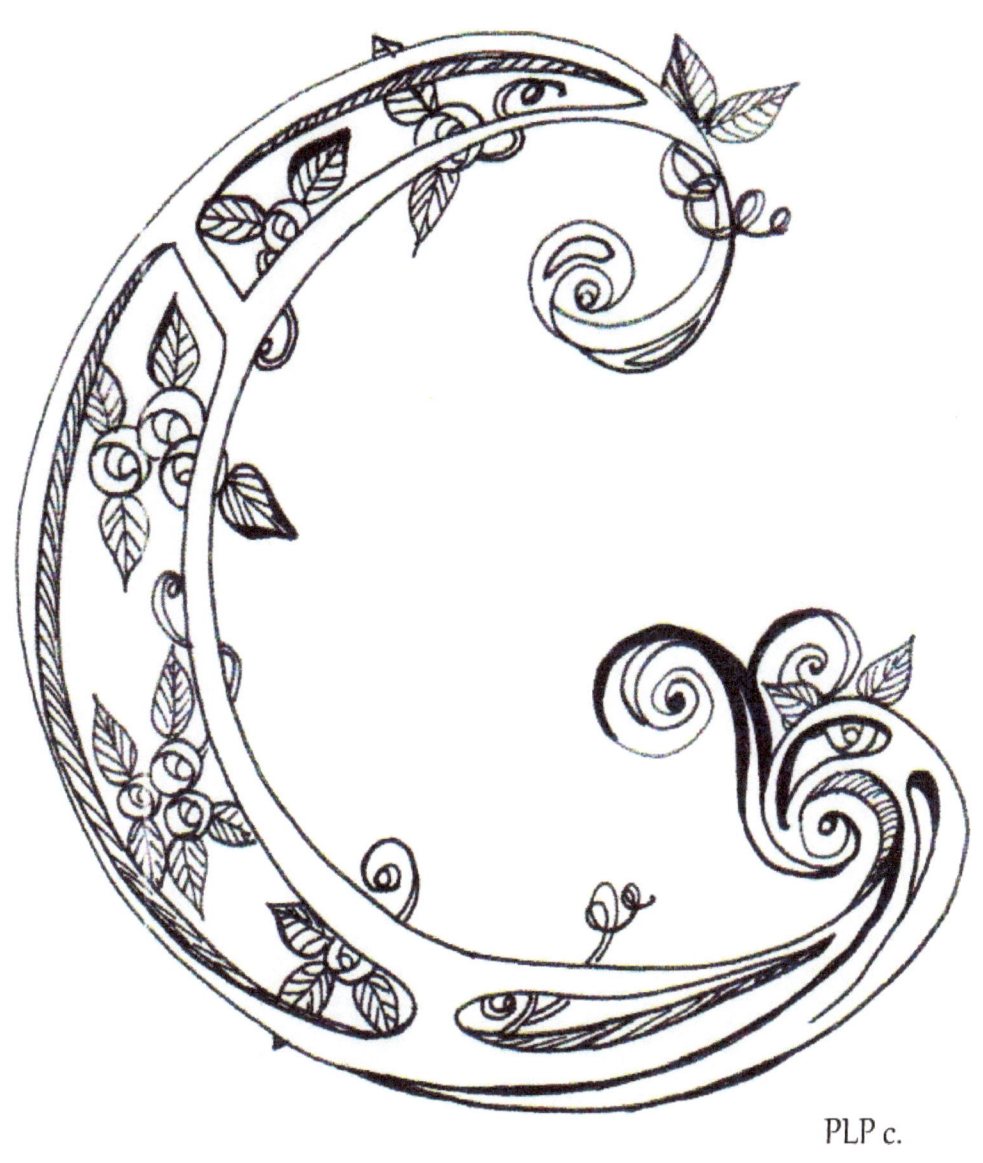

PLP c.

PLP c.

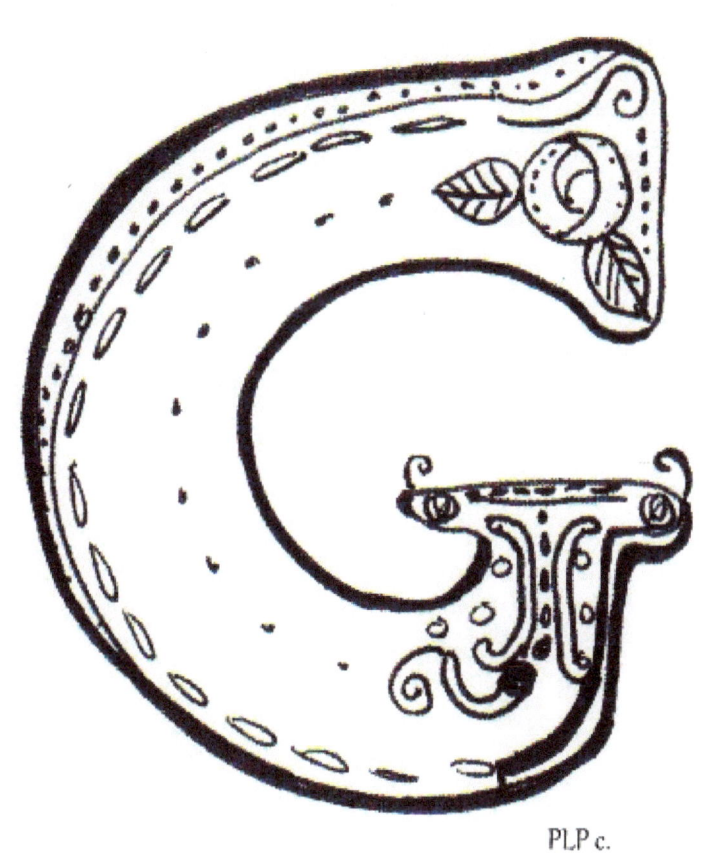

PLP c.

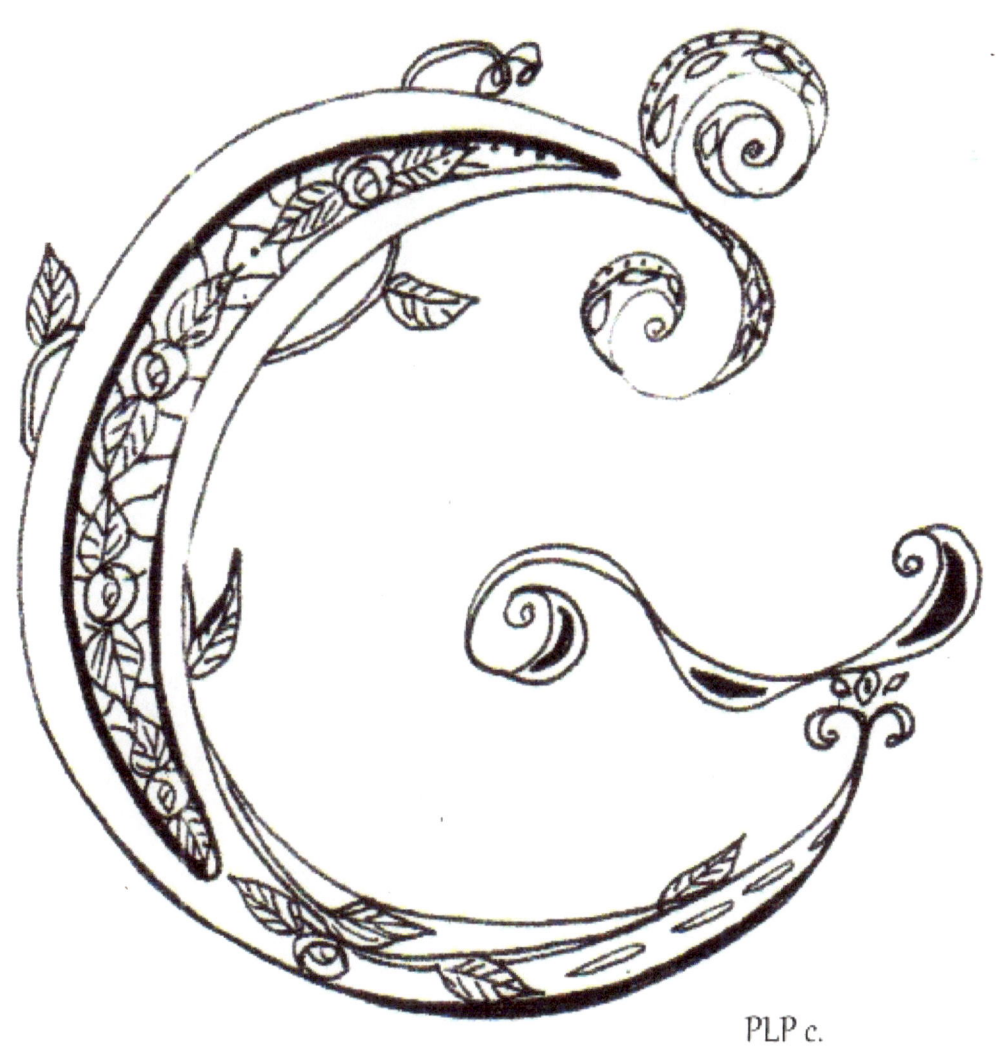

PLP c.

PLP c.

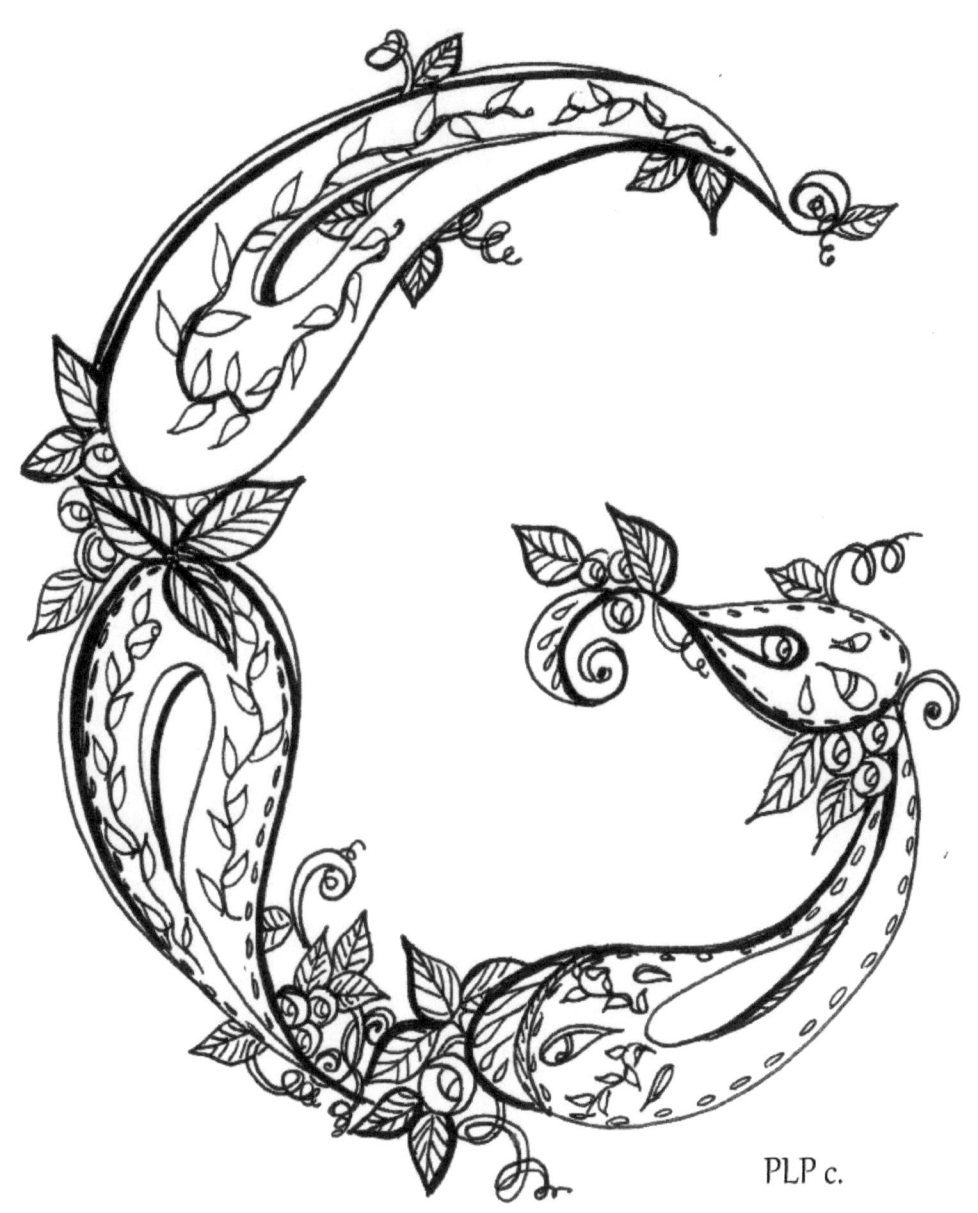

PLP c.

PLP c.

PLP c.

PLP c.

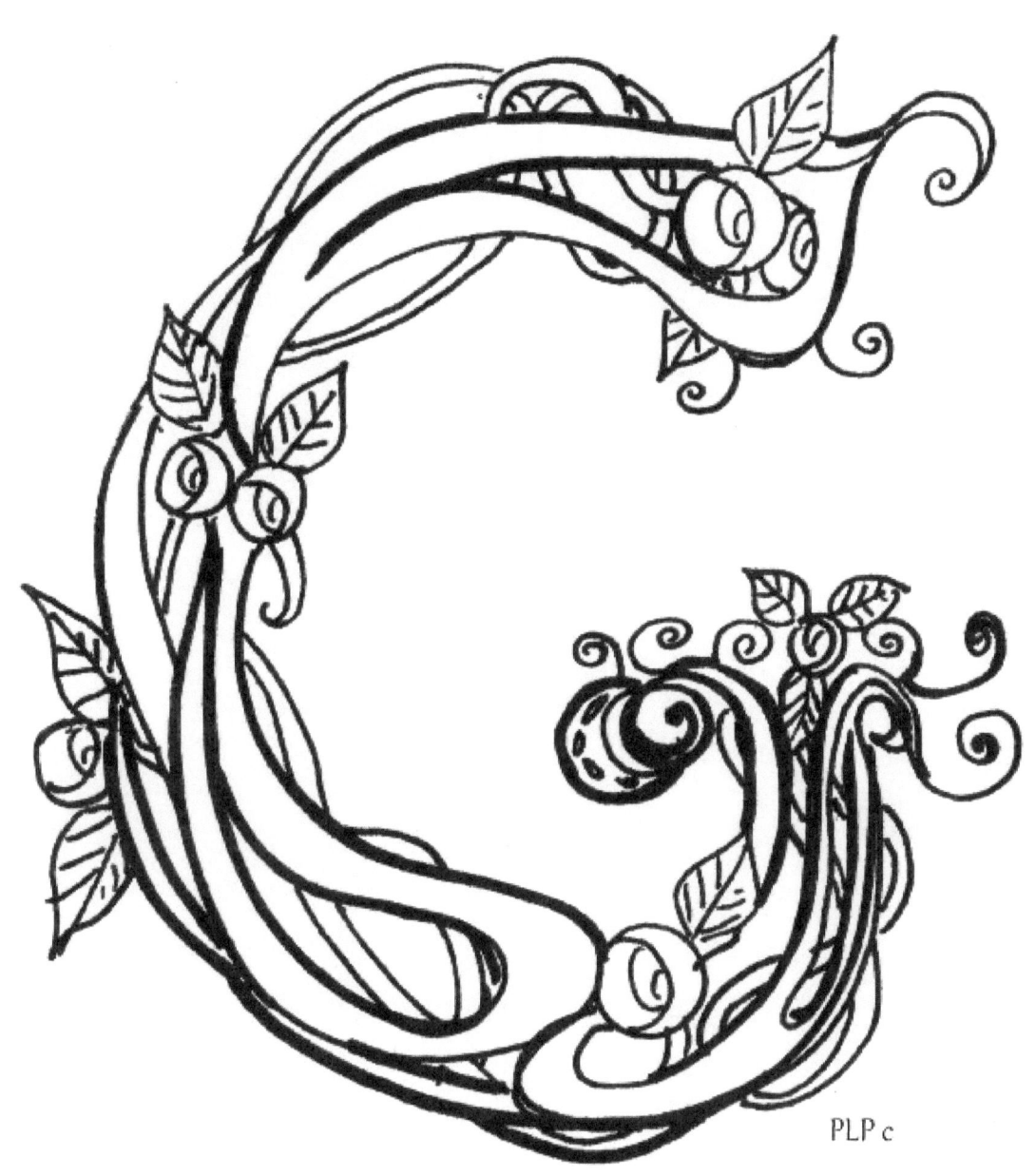

PLP c

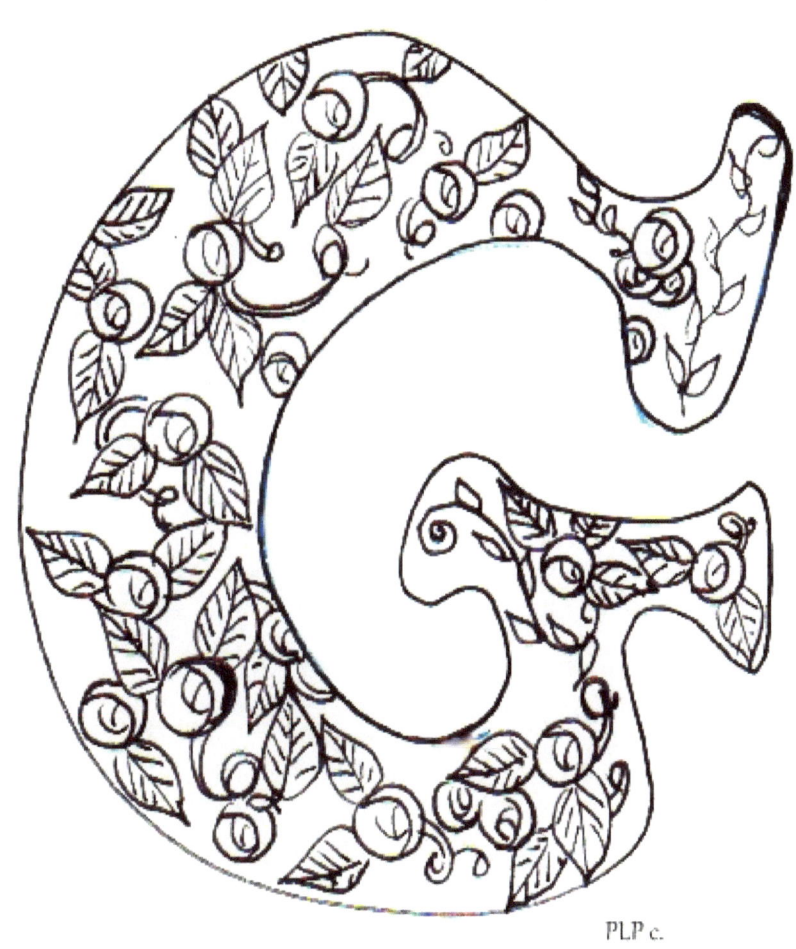

PLP c.

Can you make this G look like Bandana and Rope ?

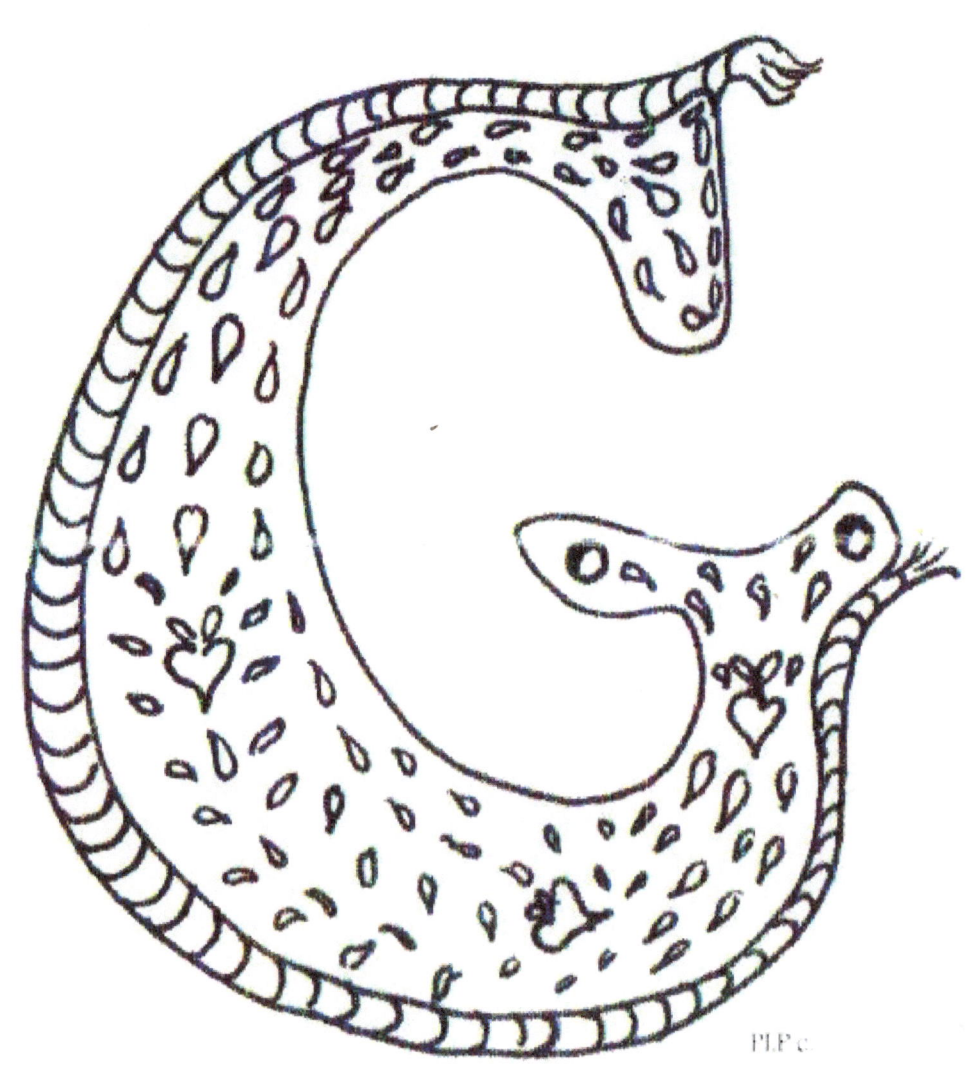

How many of the Gs you colored can you find in the next page? Which are your favorites? Why not free hand draw one of your own letter Gs......

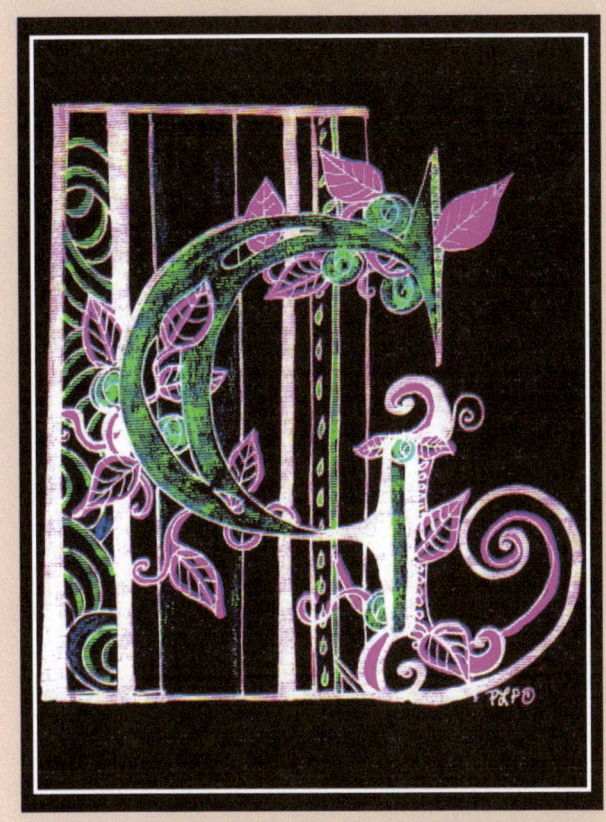

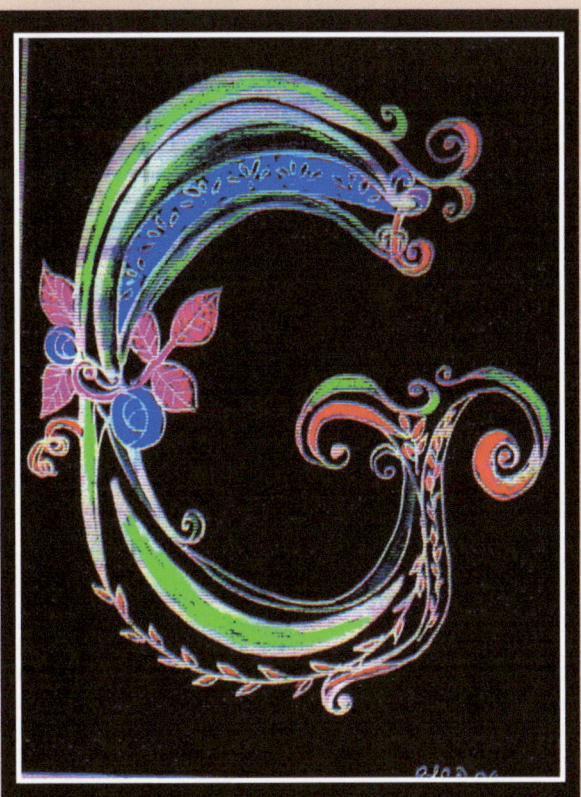

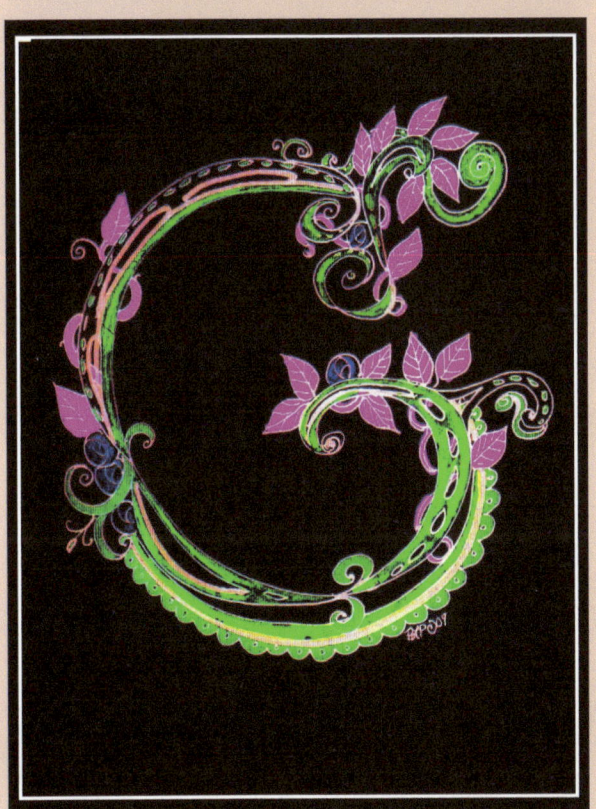

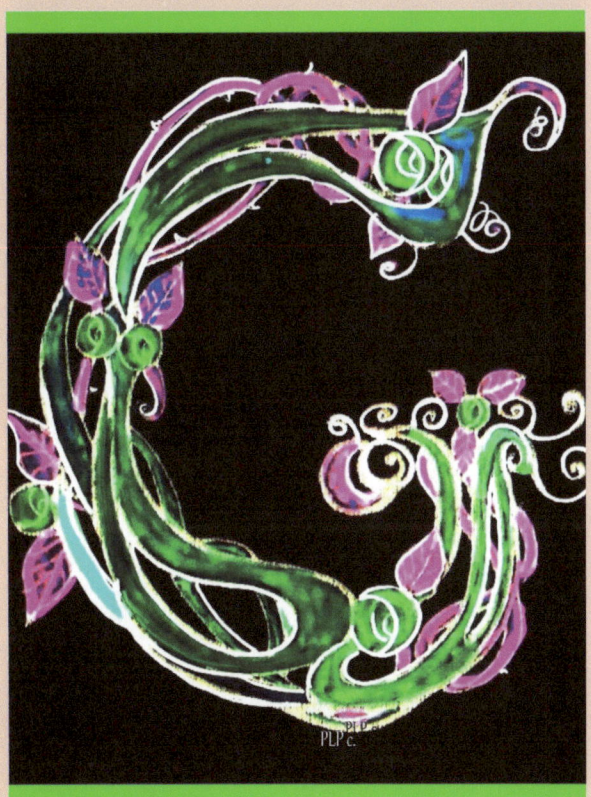